My Family and Other Superheroes

JONATHAN EDWARDS

SEREN

Seren is the book imprint of
Poetry Wales Press Ltd.
57 Nolton Street, Bridgend, Wales, CF31 3AE
www.serenbooks.com
facebook.com/SerenBooks
Twitter:@SerenBooks

The right of Jonathan Edwards to be identified as
the author of this work has been asserted in accordance
with the Copyright, Designs and Patents Act, 1988.

ISBN: 978-1-78172-162-9
ISBN: kindle: 978-1-78172-164-3
ISBN:e-book: 978-1-78172-163-6

A CIP record for this title is available from the British Library.

The publisher acknowledges the financial assistance of the Welsh Books Council.

Cover painting: 'Cock-a-Hoop' by James Donovan, http://jamesdonovanart.com/

Printed in Bembo by Bell & Bain Ltd, Glasgow.

Contents

1

2

3

4

1

My Family in a Human Pyramid

My uncle starts it, kneeling in his garden;
my mother gives a leg up to my gran.
When it's my turn to climb, I get a grip
of my bamp's miner's belt, my cousin's heels,
say *Thank you* for her birthday card as I go,
then bounce on my nan's perm and skip three rows,
land on my father's shoulders. He grabs my ankles,
half holding me up and half holding me close.

Here he comes, my godson, Samuel Luke,
passed up until he's standing in his nappy
on my head. And now to why we're here:
could the Edwardses together reach a height
that the youngest one of us could touch a star?
Sam reaches out. He points towards the night.

Evel Knievel Jumps Over my Family

A floodlit Wembley. Lisa, the producer,
swears into her walkie-talkie. We Edwardses,
four generations, stand in line,
between ramps: *Smile for the cameras.*

My great-grandparents twiddle their thumbs
in wheelchairs, as Lisa tells us to relax,
Mr Knievel has faced much bigger challenges:
double-deckers, monster trucks, though the giraffe

is urban legend. Evel Knievel enters,
Eye of the Tiger drowned by cheers,
his costume tassels, his costume a slipstream,
his anxious face an act to pump the crowd,

surely. My mother, always a worrier,
asks about the ambulance. Evel Knievel
salutes, accelerates towards the ramps.
I close my eyes, then open them:

is this what heaven feels like,
some motorcycle Liberace overhead,
wheels resting on air? Are these flashes
from 60,000 cameras the blinding light

coma survivors speak of? Before he lands,
there's just time to glance along the line:
though no one's said a thing,
all we Edwardses are holding hands.

Gregory Peck and Sophia Loren
in Crumlin for the Filming of *Arabesque*,
June 1965

Sunday. The crowd beneath the viaduct
waves banners made from grocery boxes, bedsheets:
Welcome to the valleys Mr Peck!
Wind turns their chapel dresses into floral
parachutes; their perms don't budge an inch.
The emotion of it's too much for one girl's
mascara. *We love you Miss Loren!* My father

parks away from them, around the corner,
in his brand new car, a '30s Lanchester,
with stop-start brakes, a battery he shares
with a neighbour. All sideburns and ideas, a roll-up
behind one ear and a flea in the other
from my gran for missing Eucharist,
he coughs and steps down from the running board,

as two Rolls-Royces pull up opposite.
Gregory Peck, three years after being
Atticus Finch, steps from one, says *Good morning*.
From the other – it isn't! – it *is*, wearing her cheekbones.
My father's breakfast is nervous in his stomach,
but he grabs his *Argus*, pen, and *Yes*, they'll sign.
Her high heels echo away through the whole valley.

That's how my father tells it. Let's gloss over
how his filming dates aren't quite the same as Google's,
the way Sophia Loren formed her Ss
suspiciously like his. Let's look instead
at this photo of the crowd gathered that day,
he walked towards to share those autographs,
his fame. There, front and middle, with her sister,

the girl he hasn't met yet – there. My mother.

The Voice in which my Mother Read to Me

isn't her good morning, good afternoon, good night voice,
her karaoke as she dusts, make furniture polite voice,
her saved for neighbours' babies and cooing our dog's name voice.

It isn't her best china, not too forward, not too shy voice,
or her dinner's ready, your room looks like a sty voice,
or her whisper in my ear as she adjusts my tie voice.

It's not her roll in, Friday night, *Lucy in the Sky* voice,
her Sunday morning, smartest frock, twinkle-in-the-eye voice,
that passing gossip of the vicar with the Communion wine voice.

It's not her 'Gateau – no, ice cream – no… I can't make
                                    the choice' voice.
It's not her decades late, fourth change, 'Is this skirt
                                    smart enough?' voice.
It's not her caught me with the girl from number twenty-one voice.

That voice which she reserved for twelve-foot grannies,
                                    Deep South hobos,
that sleepy, secret staircase, selfish giants, Lilliput voice.
That tripping over, 'Boy, why is your house so full of books?' voice.

The Death of Doc Emmett Brown
in *Back to the Future*

I sit here in the darkness with my father,
slurping Pepsi, passing popcorn round.
The Libyans come fast around the corner,

pump Doc Brown with automatic fire.
My feet are dangling, inches from the ground.
I sit here in the darkness with my father,

as Marty hits 88 miles an hour,
goes back to '55, to warn Doc Brown.
The Libyans come fast around the corner,

pump Doc Brown with automatic fire:
he gets up, dusts his bulletproof vest down.
I sit here in the darkness with my father,

who starts to gently snore. Now time goes quicker:
the cinema's knocked down, moved out of town;
the Libyans come fast around the corner

on DVD. My boy asks for *Transformers*
instead as, from the wall, his bamp looks down.
I sit here in the darkness with my father.
The Libyans come fast around the corner.

Half-time, Wales vs. Germany, Cardiff Arms Park, 1991

Nil-nil. Once the changing room door's closed,
the Germans out of sight, the Welsh team can
collapse: there's Kevin Ratcliffe, belly up
on the treatment table; Sparky Hughes's body
sulks in the corner, floppy as the curls

which he had then. All half, they've barely had
a kick. Big Nev Southall throws his gloves
to the floor, like plates in a Greek restaurant
as, in tracksuit and belly, Terry Yorath
looks round at a room of Panini faces:

he doesn't know yet he will never get them
to a major finals. He does know what to say.
Ryan Giggs, still young enough to be
in a boy band, stands up, doing an impression
of his poster on my wall. The crowd begins

to ask for guidance from the great Jehovah
and Ian Rush's famous goal-scoring
moustache perks up. He's half an hour away
from the goal that cues the song that makes his name
five syllables. What he doesn't know

is I'm in the stand in my father's coat,
storing things to tell at school next day.
My father pours more tea from his work flask
and says *We got them now butt, watch* and asks
again if I'm too cold. What we don't know

is we'll speak of this twenty years from now –
one of us retired, one a teacher –
in a stadium they'll build down by the river.
But now it's Rushie Sparky Southall Giggs.
8.45: the crowd begins to roar,

wants to be fed until they want no more.
The tea tastes just like metal, is too hot
and something catches – right here – on the tongue.
The changing room door opens and they step out,
toe-touching, stretching, blinking under floodlights –

it's time to be the people we'll become.

How to Renovate a Morris Minor

That's him, in the camouflage green overalls,
hiding under the car all day from my mother.
What is he but a pair of feet, my father,

muttering prayers to God and the sump gasket,
wearing oil drips, enough zips for all
his secrets? On his back, he pokes a spanner

up at a nut, as if unscrewing heaven;
grease-fingers make a crime scene of the kitchen.
He gives the stars in his bucket to the bonnet

and when he sees his face in it then it
is smiling. His foot on the accelerator
makes the world go, his right arm at the auction

can't say *No* and when the day is over,
that's him, that's him – he's snoring on the sofa,
Practical Classics open on his lap –

his eyes dart under their lids as he sleeps,
like Jaguars he's racing in his dreams.

Bamp

That's him, with the tweed and corduroy
skin, wearing the slack gloves of his hands,
those liver spots like big full stops. That's him

passing time with his favourite hobby, which is
you know, pottering, or staring closely
at the middle distance, enjoying the magic tricks

his watch does. His pockets are for special things
he has forgotten, no one fills the holes
in crumpets like he does, and in his wallet

is a licence from the Queen and what it means
is he can say what the hell he likes and you
can't do nothing. That's him, with a cupboard full

of tea cosies, a severe hearing problem
round those he doesn't like, gaps in his smile
and stories, a head full of buried treasure

and look, that's him now, twiddling his thumbs
so furiously, it's like he's knitting air.
It's only him can hold the air together.

Building my Grandfather

He comes flat-pack, a gift for my eighteenth.
We tip the bits out on the living room carpet:
nuts and bolts, a spanner, an Allen key,
tubes halfway between telescopes and weapons.
At first he goes together easily:
slippered left foot clicks into the ankle,
shin joins at a perfect right angle.
We have more of a problem with the right knee,
but my father remembers it was always gammy
from twelve-hour shifts, labouring in tight seams.
I fit the lungs, pumping in mustard gas
which filled each breath he took from 1918.
Something seems to be missing from the heart
and for a while we search beneath the sideboard,
but then my father says it's probably
for the old man's brother, who joined up when he did
and didn't make it back. The cheek and neck
and nose slot in and soon, we've almost got him:
my father holds the lips, the final bit
before he opens his eyes and I meet him.
A glance in the mirror at what he's going to see:
a pale-faced boy by an electric fire,
Nike swoosh like a medal on my chest.
It's then I say *Stop*. What will he make of me?

Lance Corporal Arthur Edwards (1900–1916)

You took the River Ebbw to the Somme
in your canteen, and never brought it back,
but it's still there, each time I look out my window.
I picture you there, holding the bottle under
to catch the water which proved you'd make it home.
Mid-river, stooping, shorter than your shadow,
your Sunday trousers are rolled up to your knees
so your mam won't kill you. A sixteen-year-old flamingo.

Now your face is blown up, above our mantelpiece;
you're prey to the latest image manipulation.
Your eyes are horror movies'; your eyes are God's.
You're close to the portrait of your elder brother
as he was to you when the blast hit. You look like each other:
his painted face is a sorry imitation.

My Uncle Walks to Work, 1962

He has a summer job as a postman,
so races up at six. In the living room,
my gran is poking the fire, cursing my grandad
who'll die before I'm born.

Out of the house and down the hill,
past The Crown, sometimes repenting the night before.
He rounds the corner by the block of flats,
or would do but it isn't there yet,

into the sorting office,
knocked down when I was a kid.
He shoulders his bag of mail
and staggers back up the hill,

into his street, into his house,
my gran still poking and cursing,
up the stairs. He drops the sack on the bedroom floor
(careful not to wake my father

who has to get up for work in an hour)
and goes back to bed.
He'll do the delivery when he's properly rested.
Let him sleep. He has much ahead of him:

a bag of mail, a wife, three children,
five (and counting) grandkids
and every year he buys me a hardback copy
of the winner of the Booker Prize.

2

Anatomy

These shoulder blades are Snowdon, the Brecon Beacons.
Walk gently on them. This spine is the A470;
these palms are Ebbw, Wye, Sirhowy. This tongue

is Henry VIII's Act of Union, these lungs
pneumoconiosis, these rumbling guts
the Gurnos, this neck Dic Penderyn. This manner

of speaking is my children, my children's children.
These vital organs are Nye Bevan, this liver
Richard Burton, this blood my father. These eyes

have been underground for generations; now
they're adjusting to the light. This gap-toothed smile
is the Severn Bridge, seen from the English side.

View of Valleys Village from a Hill

From here you see how small it is, how narrow:
terraced houses gone square-eyed from looking
too long at the homes opposite, while people
lug their lives to bus stop, chip shop, chapel.
From here, I could reach down

and fuck with them. Look, here comes my sister
with her latest bloke. Watch now as I take
his hair between thumb and forefinger and gently
pull: his eyebrows rise in shock, as if
to compensate. From here,

you feel the way God feels if God is
lonely: it's all wind blow-drying the grass
for its big night out, radio-friendly birdsong,
sheep doing their thought balloon impressions.
From here, I could destroy everyone I know
by blinking. From here, I could step off

the world. My father comes out of the shop,
cracking a rolled-up *Argus* against his hip,
doing the walk I nicked from him.
He lights a cigarette mam can't stub out:

from here I'll see him safely home,
scan miles around for speeding cars,
watch his breath rise through the air,
disappear before it reaches here.

View of Valleys High Street through a Café Window

Out there, policemen in attention-seeking
fluoro-vests eye up a single mam
pushing a pram, her head down and her face
so much a frown, it's like she's trying to mow

the pavement. Brollies bob above each head
like thought balloons, if everyone were thinking,
Fuck me, it's raining. They're not thinking that,
these lovers who hold hands at just the height

of shopping bags, or this girl who smokes a fag
and rides a bike past, like a really crap
steam train. A man with a cumulonimbus
beard enters a phone box and I wait

for him to emerge as Superman. He checks
the tray for change, as his hot-water bottle
wags its tail. In this window, our ghosts,
those silly sods, sit at the pavement table,

eating cake from their left hands and getting
soaked. A board outside the travel agent's
puts a price on the sun. The democratic
rain falls on it, on them, on everyone.

Colliery Row

That's it, with the bloke at number five,
whose days are driving buses, nights The Crown.
To watch him walking down the street at night's
to forecast how his bus will be next day:
if he's wobbling, then you'd best stay in the house,
but if he's walking straight, you'll be okay.

At number six? The terrace's *Don Juan*.
At the first sign of sunshine he's half-naked
on a deck chair out front with a beer can.
His belly over his shorts is a landslide
which traps for days a hillside family cottage,
a school, a church, an entire alpine village,

but no women. Not even her across the road,
our lady on the other side of the curtains,
who's been walking around beneath a cloud
of dark hair since she watched her husband go.
Her car is parked outside all summer, pointing
away from here. She looks out through the window

at skateboard kids, who run rings round my childhood,
making ramps of bits of brick and wood,
so they can take off, shake off this old street
for an instant. They land outside number three,
Jasmine Cottage, all *Neighbourhood Watch*,
all *No Parking Here Please* and untouched

daughters. The bloke at the other end of the row
carried hods and now he's carrying
his unemployment. In his garden grow
For Sale signs. Today, he's out back, burning something —
his smoke signals to neighbours translate,
roughly, as *Screw you!* At number eight's

the stately home of a terraced princess,
whose fake tan really turns her into someone
from somewhere else. She lets down her hair
for a Friday night hero, an ear-pierced bloke,
a handbrake magician, all mouth and sound system,
whose car disappears in a puff of smoke.

The terraced houses, semi-detached lives.
What is a street for? Wind picks up, tonight,
and a bus driver sways towards his home.
The stars come out above Colliery Row,
as far as stars from anywhere on earth.
Look up at them now. Imagine living here.

USA Family Kebab House,
Merthyr Tydfil

Only the counter stands between them:
on the left, Gloria, shifting her fatness
from hip to hip, as if it were a baby,

on the right, him. She knows each move by now:
his body tight as he reaches with the knife,
slices the pole-dancing doner, dips his fingers

in the needless salad. Customer service
is love: *Have a good evening, pretty lady.*
She knows his shifts, his favourite football team

and where he lives. Back home,
she can't wait for knives and forks,
shuffles some bills into a table mat,

lets chilli sauce drip down her chin.
Tomorrow's his day off: she'll need to be up early.
She opens a can, raises it to him.

Owen Jones

You'll find him standing sentry outside the bookies,
his reflection in the Oxfam window:
a roll-up and a cup of plastic tea.
His dreams are scribbled on papers in his pockets.

Or you'll see him, nights, in the kebab shop:
he swallows your drunk chat, counts your money
carefully into the till, ladles chilli sauce,
ekes out enough for the next day's races.

Some remember the boy he was:
how he could play off scratch at seventeen,
the trial he had for Cardiff City.
Others mention his best mate and his missis.

2.15: he flicks his fag out, goes in again,
where his clothes, his cars, his years have already been.
No one would notice his smile as the door swings.
A crisp packet rustles its applause in the wind.

Raskolnikov in Ebbw Vale

I was with my missis when I first spotted him,
down Festival Park, doing some shopping.
In his whole wardrobe, on coat-hanger bones,
he looked like some survivor of rationing
or the grunge generation, and when he spoke
there was a taste of something European.
His face was a mess of guilt and tension.

The next time was down the Rugby Club disco.
He seemed to have moved on to Joy Division,
spasm-dancing to Wham! in his coat –
his hair, cut shorter, made him look taller.
I didn't cop off, so followed him home.
He gave me the slip around by the station,
but by then I'd invented a life story for him:

how he'd survived existential angst
and a Siberian prison camp
to come to Wales, drawn to our hills –
a welcome escape from industrialisation –
and our more moderate socialism.
It was obvious to anyone who looked at him.
The next step was to have a word with him.

I was given a tip by my mate Parker,
who'd seen him come out of a flat by The Star.
I filled up the flask and tobacco tin,
parked the van in a discreet location
and settled in. It was almost morning
when he got back. I walked towards him:
it was then I felt the rock in my pocket,

my hand becoming a fist around it.

X16

The 7.54 to Cardiff is a dream.
In his shop window,
the bus driver is an ugly mannequin.

I take my seat among the regulars:
him who wakes five minutes before his stop;
her who's reading *Anna Karenina* for breakfast.

I fill in the blanks, write their lives:
she does tae kwon do on a Thursday evening;
he does the washing-up while listening to Bruce Springsteen.

That girl who got on one day
with a goldfish in a plastic bowl –
this is the third day she hasn't caught the bus.

A *Bless you*, a borrowed tissue.
At the station, we walk away from each other,
flicking cigarette ash, leaving a trail of breadcrumbs.

Chartist Mural, John Frost Square, Newport

This tunnel is the way from one place
to another: short-cutting from the station,
you pass these men, flattened by history
to a buskers' backdrop, marching for centuries
towards a Westgate they will never reach;
and bottom right, these three, forever dying,
are bleeding from their mouths, their hearts, red tiles.

This tunnel is the way from one time
to another: the school-trip boy who stares
for a morning at the unmoving men,
their fault-line features and their jigsaw jaws,
makes sketches in his head he'll never finish –
king's men firing the slowest bullets in the world
at those whose screams shatter their faces into pieces.

This tunnel traps the wind, makes catwalk models
of the men chasing Monday morning through it:
bank workers, weekend deserters, with long memories
in their laptops. Now this tramp, his duvet
growing from his chin, wondering how he got here,
wakes face-to-face with a universal manhood suffrage banner.
These bits-and-pieces men look at each other.

Capel Celyn

No one was killed here.
A military operation:
clipboards, walkie-talkies,
radar, body warmth.
They took away the gravestones.

A kind of utopia
where every shop sells fish,
public transport is scuba diving,
the crime rate zero.
Humane Pompeii, bathetic Armageddon.

In the lake, this drowned town
I would have been born in,
I see this other me, trapped, forever drowning.
And, in Liverpool, there must be something –
some taste as vague and definite as water.

In John F. Kennedy International Airport,

a toothy blonde, whose name tag said *Lucille*,
served me at check-in. I showed my ticket, was surprised
when she said, 'That's been cancelled. Sorry, sir.'
'The flight to Cardiff's off?' I said. 'It can't be, can it?'
'No sir,' she said, 'you don't quite understand. Wales
has been cancelled. It no longer exists.'

'What?!' I said. 'What do you mean, Wales doesn't exist?'
'Sir, do try and calm down,' said Lucille.
'The US Government has simply decided Wales
doesn't exist. You can hardly be surprised.
For God's sake, you guys never even made it
to the soccer World Cup finals. But don't worry, sir:

just for the convenience of clients like you, sir,
we've re-created the essential Welsh existence
in a small museum in Kansas. You'll just love it.
Male voice choirs sing *Calon Lân*,' beamed Lucille,
'as bonneted crones serve cawl-and-Welsh cake surprise,
and there are satellite link-ups with the King of Wales,

Tom Jones, and his sister, Catherine Zeta, direct from Wales
via LA. Now, could you please stop crying, sir?'
I glanced round the airport: it was full, to my surprise,
of Welshmen, mourning their land which didn't exist.
Wrapped in Welsh flags, girls ten times lusher than Lucille
asked each other where to they could score a hit

of cyanide, as men opened paracetamol, dropped it
into duty-free vodka, blubbing for Wales.
Dazed, I watched the next passenger approach Lucille
and her say, 'I'm sorry, that's been cancelled, sir.'
This guy's suit was that quality they say no longer exists,
a daffodil in his lapel, so I was surprised,

when he heard Wales had been cancelled, he flashed a surprised
smile. When she told him they'd re-created it
in Kansas, he danced a jig, laughing, 'Wales doesn't exist!'
That face looked familiar – who was this betrayer of Wales?
As she told him, 'We'll switch you to the Hawaii flight, sir,'
I leaned in to hear and that was when she said it, old Lucille:

'Our apologies again that Wales no longer exists.
What an honour and surprise to serve you. Please, call me Lucille.
Now I hope it's a pleasant flight, Mr First Minister, sir.'

FA Cup Winners on Open Top Bus Tour of my Village

I was down the park with my boy, having a kick about, when it came round the corner. Even from that distance, there was no mistaking the Versace smile of the star striker, the fairy-tale jaw of the captain. And was that the manager, cheeks red as the last inch of wine in the bottle, drunk at sunset in a hillside town in the South of France, from where you could look down on the world like you owned it?

Within minutes, the village was gathered: fathers and sons chanting grown men's names, sisters and mothers touching up make-up and cleavage. The players looked scared. The driver scratched his head, fiddled with the sat nav. Then Paul, a legend round here since losing his job, giving all his time to the Under 10s, forced his way on board, holding his son's autograph book like a begging bowl. We watched with amazement, then with anger, as the Chilean winger – the one you'd recognise from the Nike billboard – raised his fist to Paul and floored him. Suddenly, everyone was holding something: a rake, a mop, a Stanley knife, a car bumper. We went for the tyres, then the windows.

As the judge said later, in the absence of CCTV, and given the unreliable nature of witness statements, it's impossible to decide on responsibility. But let's just say this: it's easy to imagine, isn't it, what it would feel like to hold the FA Cup over your head, then bring it down – *crack!* – on twenty million quid's worth of right ankle, as the man you've been in love with for five years shakes and begs for mercy beneath you?

3

Girl

That girl's the girl I mean. That one now, wearing
no-animals-were-harmed-in-making-these-
leopardskin leggings, ears posing the question

of what are ears for, really,
but bearing the weight of the biggest silver-
coloured hoops on earth? In diamanté

scarlet heels, six inch,
when she walks, everything sparkles, everything
limps. Her hair is piled up on her head,

like the kind of coastal clifftop rampart
cameras swoop in at from the sea,
in historical action movies, featuring

Mel Gibson. Up her sleeve
is a tattoo, a Chinese symbol, and what it means
is clear. Look, that's her now, outside The Mermaid,

going a little cross-eyed as she draws
on a cigarette and shouts across the street,
asks an acquaintance if she'd like

some, would she? So how else
can I put it? How much clearer can I be?
That girl's the girl. That girl's the girl for me.

Welsh National Costume

Fancy dress? Always a laugh. My Tom Jones
sideburns-and-flares number in the bag,
we're drawn past Britney, Cinderella,
to a rail at the back. The pleats, the hat,

the lace. Your face. And later, the text you send:
Helpless. Help. I rush round to find
you're a ball of tartan on your carpet,
a post-match, post-pub Scotsman, so

I dress you. The rule of thumb
is wherever I see a bit of body,
cover it with rough checked rug:
where there are bedclothes, tablecloths,

put them on, until you're mummified
by plaid. Hold it together with safety pins
and what my mother said. *This is murder
on my skin*, you moan, but I stick to it:

the peepshow frills, the death-bell bonnet,
tied with ribbon that makes your chin
a present. Now you're all dressed:
your body's imaginary, legs an idea,

and under all that cotton, what's the self?
The only way to get you back's to hug you
and it's then I feel it, down past all those layers
of cloth and history, the light, the dark:

the steady thrum, my love, of your English heart.

Us

Me on a three-day crash course in the language
of rail travel – floors are called chairs
and chairs are called beds – to show up at your door,
eighteen years to the minute since you were born.
Your face, as if
you'd opened the door to a six-foot bottle of milk.

Me buying pearls till your neck smiles,
then nicking them, pawning them, going to the dogs.
Me learning your language – the textbook a spittoon,
the consonants rattling like an abacus.
You, with your ears stoppered
with headphones, a giant medicine bottle.

Me putting my mouth where my money is,
hurting my knees and showing you the ring,
the shop assistant's home number
scribbled on the back of the receipt.
You, with your mouth so closed,
it's a buttonhole beneath your nose.

The Doll

I woke up with my arm round my wife,
the clock somewhere between four and five,
slipped out of bed and dressed in the dark.
Paused for the rhythm of her breathing,
quick-quick-slow across the landing,
muffled the door, set off for the park,

where night had turned off all the colours –
grey-black grass and grey-black flowers.
The swings took the piss out of the gallows
and the climbing frame held up the sky.
No child swung and no child climbed.
I found her stretched beneath the willows:

about the size of a healthy baby,
dress somewhere between a sneeze and a hankie,
here-and-now lips and elsewhere eyes.
Each cheek was red as a stop sign,
on her wood wood face on wood wood bones.
Who could have left her here? Who could have known?

In the crook of my arm I carried her home,
as dawn painted its watercolour,
made a sundial of each street light.
Before I got back I'd have to drop her
and never never make mention of her,
or of the reasons I walk out at night.

Decree Nisi

Kelly, this week I've filled the house with strange men:
the plumbers and plasterers, the 'leccies and lackeys,
the lofty young shifters and shifty old lifters,
the chippies and butties, the world and his mate.
The cash-in-hand, the big white van
blocking natural light to the living room.
The painters in white overalls, the strip
they wear when drinking tea for England.

Kelly, this week I've filled the house with strange things.
Stepladders and handshakes, buckets with holes in:
I make a wish and throw the hourly rate in.
The settee's on the lawn, a madman's garden swing,
paintbrushes take up leg room in the sock drawer
and a hammer sneaks in with the knives and forks.
A photo of your mother's face down in the toilet;
dustsheets make ghosts of the tables and sideboard.

At ten to five they call it a day,
promise to be here bright and early.
I abracadabra the TV from under our old bedsheet,
settle down to a plate of leftover digestives.
It's then, Kel,
when the stars come out in the curtainless windows
and the telly echoes through my home.
It's then I say your name.

Jack-in-the-Box

Just when I think I've forgotten you,
they play that song on the radio,
or, sorting through junk, I come across photos:
you've sprung up again,
with your made-up grin, your stupid little hat.

With a school compass I gouge and scrape,
give you a Hitler moustache, a Glasgow smile,
then shut you up, lock you in.
As I'm fiddling with the matches,
you bounce up, prettier than ever.

I try the doll with long blonde hair,
who'll never give me the silent treatment
so long as I pull that string in her back.
But she doesn't have your spiral-staircase neck,
your irrepressible energy.

I snap and show up at your door.
You invite me in for coffee.
In the living room, there's a box, about my size:
you place a hand on my head,
push down against my suddenly springy legs.

The Bloke in the Coffee Shop

is a bloke and where he is is yes, you know,
a coffee shop. The bloke in the coffee shop

is what he is; he has in front of him
a coffee and his problems. *She's late again,*

he thinks, although he doesn't have a watch
and it is now, precisely. This bloke has

problems, yes, but let's forget all that:
today is Saturday and not a day

for problems. If you saw him from above,
you'd see his hair, his coffee. You wouldn't see

his problems, would you? Also, you'd be tall,
so let's forget all that. Let us instead

describe him. Let's make a heroic effort,
pin him down with a word. Now here it goes:

dark. No, that's his coffee. Our bloke's hair
is dark as well, but that's not what I meant –

What's meaning, really? thinks some bloke somewhere.
Fuck coffee, I'm off for a Guinness, I am,

thinks the dark-haired bloke in the you-know-what,
soon to be himself, but somewhere else.

★

Meanwhile, the lady walking down the street
is in the street and walking. Walking quickly,

but not so quick to make a liar of me.
Her high heels make the noise they make. Her clothes

are what she's wearing. Sure, yes, she's late,
but doesn't have a watch, or has a watch,

but hasn't time to check it, being late.
How is the weather? Pissing down. Umbrellas

hover over heads like oh-so-faithful,
massive-winged and oh yes, somehow, handled

blackbirds. So much for similes. Our lady's
just passing what she might call a boutique,

so let's look in the window now and see her.
What is she like exactly? Violently

dimpled. A handbag which contains precisely
nothing. A heartbreaking nose that's pointing

at where she's going. In short, you know, a lady:
to see her dodge round puddles is to see her

dosey doe. She makes a bloke a bloke
who's sitting in a coffee shop and waiting.

★

Who's thinking he's been stood up, actually,
so what he is is getting up and leaving,

thinking his thoughts – that's not your thoughts,
                                    his thoughts –
though if you saw his face now then your thoughts

would be *Poor bloke*. Listen, that's his best
brogues he put on just for her this morning,

after his best socks (he finds that order
sensible), making the noise they make,

as he moves to the door. What do you call that,
clomping? Forgive me: rarely could a pair

of brogues have generated quite so much
pathos. At the door, he stops to light

one of the cigarettes she doesn't like,
puffing it so violently, you'd think

he's thinking – ooh – of puffing it at her.
The rain, you say? He's getting wet? He's under

the awning, ain't he? Shows what you know, reader.
So now the bloke in the coffee shop's the bloke

outside who's looking north towards The Dog,
shuffling, smoking and not going there yet.

★

Meanwhile, the lady walking down the street
is in the street and walking. She's what, a hundred

yards away and can't see our man yet,
what with the crowds, the brollies hovering

like we said they were hovering before.
And so we come – huh *hum* – to the dramatic

part of the poem: here's our protagonist,
our love interest. It's not for me to say

which is which, things being what they are
post-feminism, post-structuralism, pre-

the Big Question. The Big Question is,
will these two meet? Now let me answer that:

watch this. The lady walking down the street
is rushing, look, so quickly to her date,

she trips and lands at the feet of our bloke
and in that instant she's thinking two things –

Aaaahhhh and *What a lovely pair of brogues.*
He helps her up, into the coffee shop,

to meet the bloke she's meeting – someone else,
some chukka-booted bloke in the coffee shop.

★

Now our bloke makes his way towards the pub
and doesn't see *his* girl again or sees her

and gives up coffee at New Year, or switches
to decaf for a bit, as his brogues slowly

wear or sit unworn in his wardrobe
and the weather brightens up or, more than likely,

doesn't. All that's in the future. Now
our lady sits recovering with a latte,

chatting to the bloke she's there to meet.
She isn't thinking of our man at all,

or is she? Is she? Not my place to say –
as I sit with espresso and a pen

and look out through the window at people passing,
so close they could reach out and touch each other –

not my place to say if she'll buy her man
a lovely pair of brogues for his next birthday,

or in this hour before the café closes,
if she'll look out at the rain and think this,

or something like this, brushing her grazed palm:
The touch. His hand. The warm touch of his hand.

Aquafit

Mondays. 7pm. The ladies
sink into the pool,
chat of their parents' health, their daughters' work.
Their bathing suits are holding something back.

Squat thrusts and shuttle runs:
they walk in the water.
The instructress stands above them like a billboard,
mimicking them: 'And right, and left, and...'.

In the men's changing room,
a boy in council uniform
sweeps the dregs of shampoo to the drain.
From the pool come love songs.

4

Bookcase Thrown through
Third Floor Window

It has *The Complete Jane Austen,*
The Nurse's Dictionary of Medicine,
and here it comes, crashing through the window.

It has *The Collected Shakespeare, The Holy Bible,*
and as it falls, books tumble from its shelves,
open out, use themselves as parachutes.

Then it hits the road.
Noise and dust everywhere.
It's tall as a dead man, a toppled sentry box.

My neighbours, my friends,
in a circle, are wielding
frying pans, rakes, brushes and mops,

closing in on the bookcase.
I grab a dustbin lid and maintain eye contact.

Restaurant where I am the Maître d'
and the Chef is my Unconscious

I put through an order for *spaghetti aglio e olio*.
He sends out a soup bowl full of blue emulsion.
A regular asks for lamb shank with rosemary.
Out comes a beetroot served with a corkscrew.
Someone I suspect of being a restaurant reviewer
orders the baked rum and chocolate pudding.
A mermaid rides a horse out of the kitchen.

He locks himself in there for days.
All I get are incoherent mumblings,
often in French. Some nights after closing time,
we sit down together with a glass or two,
get on famously, see eye-to-eye.
Next day he sits in a deck chair all through service,
wearing a paper hat and a tie-dyed surplice.

'That's it,' I say, 'I'm speaking to the owner.'
That night, he shakes me awake,
takes the lid off a serving dish:
an actual star he's taken out of the sky
and put on a plate. I know it's only a dream,
but next evening I'm bright and early at the restaurant,
shouting the orders, shaking the customers' hands,

picking bits of gold out of my teeth.

Rilke at War

The smallest uniform they make buries him
and after three weeks of paying lip service
to the parade ground's language
of grunts, its dactylic
Hup-two-three, the days of marching to
nowhere, slowly, mocked for his nancy's
middle name, the army find
the perfect place in war for him:

the archives. His office hours are nine till three
and he has the freedom of Vienna, an apartment
with window boxes, a genial
First Lieutenant. In days,
they've had to bump him down from propaganda
to card-filing, page-ruling,
but even that leaves him so exhausted,
he's in bed by eight each night and writing

nothing. Meanwhile, Europe is becoming
mud; my grandad comes back from the Somme
without a brother. Meanwhile, Rilke
sits in a patron's summer garden, drinking tea.
Tomorrow, he'll ask again about a full discharge,
but this afternoon he has his portrait painted
by a girl he cannot stand who shares his bed.
Now the china tinkles. His eyes dart up.

Seal

His eyes are deeper dark within his dark.
Corkscrewing, dipsy-doing, *allez-oop*,
he loops the loop, the water his slow-motion

world, this swimmer synchronised with himself.
He floats on his back, lying in the hammock
of his body. This is his gift, his talent: head

over heels, tail over head, unfolding,
barrel-rolling, forgetting which end of him
is which, now all is circle, all is swim.

He surfaces to bark *This rock is mine*,
lies there, breathing into November air,
smoking the Havana of himself,

munches sprats, mulling over his dance,
offers his stink, his easy-to-please hands.

The Hippo

is solo, hobo, incognito,
two boulders curving out of Dettol-murk,
in a zoo his photo advertises,
doing a sponsored sitting-still all day.
Stop being a cliché, hippo, or I won't

write a poem about you. Then you'll be sorry.
What is your body but the verb *To wallow*?
What is the water but a part of self?
Google says you can crush a Ford Sierra
between your jaws. They don't say how they test this.

Candyfloss-high boys crowd your glass, betting
they could hold their breath underwater longer,
they could leap from one boulder to the other.
I abandon you
for the giraffes, stupid as window cleaners,

the lions, sunshine with teeth,
but keep coming back:
if you were to rise, show your eyes, your mouth,
would you have Martin Sheen's mud-crazy face,
breaking smoke-water in *Apocalypse Now*?

Closing time. One last go. O please, hippo,
don't be so self-effacing, so tight-fisted.
Come on out, don't you know
we love you? Wait. Is that a flash of flesh,
a hippo peepshow, or are you still snoozing?

A little girl says, *Dad, that island's moving.*

Flamingos

Who spray-painted the swans? You dilly-dally,
    shilly-shally in the shallow end
on Meccano legs, your day a foot massage,
      curve your neck into a clothes hanger
        for your rose-hue tutu and your feather boa.

You're every little girl's dream, a shock, a flock
    of neon signs, advertising candyfloss.
Why do you blush so much? Each time you eat,
      you have to kiss the you-shaped bird who floats
        in the lake surface, steal food from its throat.

February. Outside's a place of grey
    line managers, timetabled rain, the bus.
But with your silly-billy, Vegas waitress,
      camouflage-for-a-world-of-joy body,
        Fuck that, you say, *let's all be fabulous.*

Cheerleaders

They cartwheel, high-kick, hair-flick on, all sing-song,
all pom-poms, exclamation marks at the end
of whatever their hands are saying. They're all angles,
uniformed as superheroes, in their star-spangled
skirts, their belly buttons. They drop into a huddle

to *Ra-ra-ra*, make their bodies jumping stars,
now doing the splits, now falling to their knees,
or touching cowboy boot toes to their cheeks.
Their synchronised smiles say nothing can be wrong.
A final, faultless somersault and they're gone.

In the bleachers, we sit on. A tinny tannoy. Wind
plays the tuning forks at either end of the pitch.
We make ourselves bigger with giant foam hands.
Now, here come the men with their metal helmets,
their little ball, their protective shoulder pads.

Bouncers

Undertakers' coats buttoned to their throats,
they applaud their own performance to keep warm.
Like teenage girls they shift from foot to foot,
cheeks rouged by neon signs: *The Velvet Room.*

Misers' hands buried in their pockets,
the guest list's folded up next to their wallets.
They have the miraculous visions of a prophet
over the shoulder of whoever they're talking to.

They'll drive home at three or four and wake at noon
with no hangover, wrap their fists around
the kettle, make tea for their tiny girlfriends.

But for now, it's 'Pal, there's no trainers allowed,'
as this child, leaving the theatre, points at them:
'Mummy, look at the unhappy men.'

Nun on a Bicycle

Now here she comes, rattling over cobbles,
powered by her sandals, the gentle downhill
and the grace of God. Now here she comes, her habit

what it was always waiting to become:
a slipstream. Past stop signs, the pedestrian
traffic at rush hour, the humdrum mopeds,

on a day already thirty in the shade:
with her robe fluttering like solid air,
she makes her own weather. Who could blame her,

as the hill sharpens, she picks up speed and smiles
into her future, if she interrupted
the *Our Fathers* she's saying in her head,

to say *Whee*, a gentle *Whee*, under her breath?
O cycle, Sister! Look at you now, freewheeling
through the air conditioning of the morning –

who's to say the God who isn't there
isn't looking down on you and grinning?

The Bloke Selling Talk Talk in the Arcade

He's got the patter, the natter, the gift
of the gab. He's got all the flattery
you can stand, different routines for madam
and sir, all that self-help book, cod amateur
psychology, the professional
bullshit, the *Hey, how's it goin', my man?*
He's got you eating out of the palm

of his hand. He's got the Prince Charming,
the *How are you, darlin'?*, the body language
training, the feints, the moves. He knows
the moment to run a hand through his smooth,
smooth hair, when to nod sagely, as if he
cares, understands. He's got the world
in his mobile and the pen in his

hand. He's got the opening line, the spiel,
the feel for people, knows the time
to look into your eyes, touch your
arm, to hang back, play it calm,
to open up about his life, to ask about
your children, your wife. He's got your future
waiting for you: just reach out and

take it. His brunette student sidekick
advertises herself but our man's got the pen,
the pen, an afternoon of chatting up
men, and when, at five, he packs up
his tongue for the day and walks into the world,
just like you, like me, like anyone,
he's got the air, the night, the setting sun.

Starbucks Name Tag Says *Rhian*

With her Minnie Mouse voice and her Popeye
tattoos, she is the Queen
of mug rings. Slow-stepping in sensible shoes
with that brush, she sweeps
the world before her. Her flirtatiousness
is customer service training, her complimentary
uniform an apron, her nemeses
the teenage couple in the khazi. She
takes no prisoners and does her duty,
holds the mop's head under in the bucket,
bench-presses tables, chairs, beneath
that bouffant. Sometimes you'll catch her
humming along to the piped Nina Simone,
stealing breaks to gaze out through the window,
tuck one stray hair behind an ear. Her smile
says she'll take the clouds out of the sky
to make your latte, or if she can't reach that far,
at least she'll flutter those big eyelashes
at the tip jar. Now she turns to you:
What's it to be then, sweetie? Look, the gold-toothed till
is open-mouthed again at all that beauty.

The Girls on the Make-up Counter

They stand and wait for you to want some me-time,
hairdos piled up like the Coldstream Guards:
they stand and wait to be your name-badged friends.

They come in close, intimate as opticians,
mascara brushes growing from their fingers.
Close your eyes, they whisper, as you make a wish

to look like them. They smile and smile,
working hard to get your reflection right.
They'll have to do this to themselves tonight,

stand before a mirror, breathe in their waists,
mutter something, then step into a city
where every other woman wears their face.

Karaoke

Friday nights we try out other voices:
the boy with the piercing and the *HATE* tattoo
wants us to love him tender, love him true,

stumbling over the newsreader's autocue.
The landlord asks his mam to mind the bar
while he pops round to give us *My Way*. His way.

The girl who's got every boozed-up eye in the place
would like to know if we'll still love her, tomorrow;
disco lights make a superstar of her shadow.

Next morning, I rescue overalls from the washing,
button up, slip back into my own skin,
head out to the van, start it up, and find myself whistling.

Brothers

You know the sort: they borrow each other's t-shirts,
wear each other's sweat under their armpits.
In the pub, you swear you hear one's voice and turn
to find the other chatting up your girl,
or else you catch one, curling up his lip,
as if he's trying on his brother's smile,
or you go to the bar and they both show up.
One has a knackered Transit, the other jump leads.
They've one gym membership and their own bodies,
tell the punch lines to each other's jokes
and if you're fool enough to bother one,
you'll find yourself outside with both of them.
You know the sort: the elder has a child
who's got her mother's mouth, her uncle's eyes.

The Boy with the Pump-action Water Pistol

snipes from hedges at ladies fresh for chapel,
or dribbles a ball round old man Walker's Astra
to score at Wembley. He floats above the ground
on his skateboard, plays toy dinosaurs,
lives in a land beyond time. Butterflies
outwit him: his idea of hunting is applause.
Pockets full of conkers, his head of acorns,
he raids his mother's washing line for the sail
of the pirate ship he's dreamt into the garden,
then sprints off to catch tadpoles, measles, snails.
O boy with the pump-action water pistol,
here's to your ballet ankles, crash-pad knees,
these summer days I watch you through this window.
I have been careful. No one's spotted me.

The Performance

On a quiet Tuesday in our village,
workmen started putting up a stage
in the square. When Will Johnson,
who has the butcher's there, came out
to see what all the fuss was about,
he found they spoke no English.

By noon, the news was everywhere.
Some said it was all for a performance
by travelling players, others a boxing bout
between the vicar and the mayor,
or for some visiting dignitary, like the Queen
or Wayne Rooney. What wasn't in doubt

was the expense: faux-Roman pillars,
flower arrangements camouflaging speakers,
a climbing frame lighting rig, a portable
orchestra pit. Neighbours talked about it
all afternoon, claimed indifference: the baby
to put to bed, something on the telly,

but by half-six, everyone was gathered
in their best clothes. Money changed hands
for seats in the front row, while at the back,
there was something approaching an insurrection
over whether one arse cheek means possession.
Quiet settled as the performance time came

and went, and nothing happened:
by seven-thirty we were restless and thirsty
and some fella started hawking cans of beer.
The first of us stormed the stage an hour later,
swaying slightly, ready to have a go at
an a cappella *Swing Low, Sweet Chariot,*

got a can to the cranium for his efforts.
That started it: an industrial speaker
was put through the butcher's window,
a lily was rammed down the vicar's earhole,
some kid made monkey bars of the lighting rig,
until it collapsed and smashed, setting fire

to the now obviously polystyrene pillars.
We finished up cracking the stage with our seats:
all in all, it must have made a sight
for the workmen who then came around the corner,
with their mops and brushes, their mirror ball heads,
speaking no English, whistling to themselves.

Holiday

Unable to sleep for the fourth night in a row,
I get up, say *Fuck it*, drive to the nearest hotel.
The receptionist looks twice at my pyjamas,
the hot-water bottle that's my only luggage,
but money is money, and business is business.
The room has a double bed and double pillows.
The walls are white; there's a carpet I wouldn't have chosen.
I fall asleep before I've brushed my teeth.

It works for a week. Then the porter
calls me by my name. At four that morning,
still awake, I look for the Gideon's Bible, and find
my address book in its place. The final straw
is when I hear *Room service!* at the door.
Opening it, I find, holding silver trays,
my wife and daughter, my parents and my boss,
asking me if this is what I ordered.

On the Overpass

I like the one above the local bypass,
my parents' farmhouse lit up on the hillside,
traffic rushing under at all times.
Also, the fence is dead easy to climb,

the outside ledge just deep enough to stand on.
Don't worry. Look, I'm always sure to hold on:
now with my right hand, now with my left.
I like that moment when I'm teetering

and free. This is the second time this week.
I get so bored. Listen, here's a lorry:
it goes *Woosh*. Then the wind goes *Wuh-huh*.
It's too cold to stay up here for long, really,

but I like to make up stories in my head:
is this you, lovely boy, speeding your Corsa
towards me, your friend in the passenger seat
big-eyed, looking up now through the windscreen?

Acknowledgements

Some of these poems have previously appeared in *14*, *Agenda Broadsheets*, *Cannon Poets*, *Cheval*, *The Frogmore Papers*, *The Interpreter's House*, *Iota*, *The Lightship Anthology 2*, *Magma*, *New Welsh Review*, *The North*, *nth position*, *Obsessed with Pipework*, *Orbis*, *Other Poetry*, *Planet*, *Poems for a Welsh Republic*, *Poetry Review*, *Poetry Wales*, *The Reader*, *Red Poets*, *The Rialto*, *Roundyhouse*, *Smiths Knoll*, *The Stinging Fly* and *The Warwick Review*.

Some of these poems were included in a collection which won the Terry Hetherington Award in 2010. I am very grateful to Alan and Jean Perry, Aida Birch and Amanda Davies.

'Evel Knievel Jumps Over my Family' won second place in the Cardiff International Poetry Competition 2012. 'Gregory Peck and Sophia Loren in Crumlin for the Filming of *Arabesque*, June 1965' was commended in the Basil Bunting Award 2012. 'Brothers' won third prize in the Cannon Poets Sonnet Competition 2012. 'How to Renovate a Morris Minor' won first prize in the Newark Poetry Competition 2012. 'Bamp' was commended in the flamingofeather poetry competition 2013.

The author wishes to acknowledge the award of a New Writer's Bursary from Literature Wales in 2011, for the purpose of completing this collection.

Thank you: Saskia Barnden; David Briggs, David Clarke and the members of the Bristol Poetry School; Michael Hulse, David Morley and the staff and students of the Warwick Writing Programme; Mike Jenkins and the Red Poets; and Amy Wack and everyone at Seren. Thank you beyond measure to my parents.